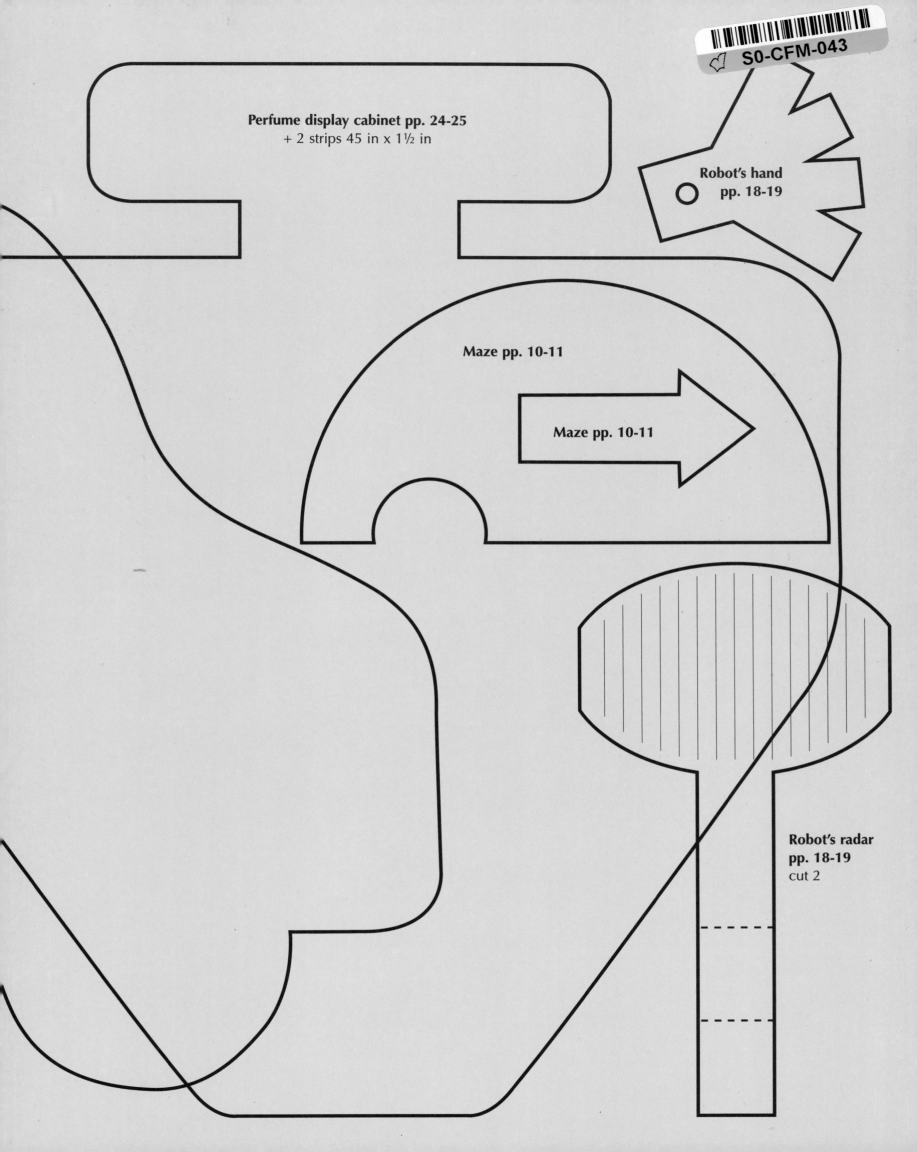

Perfume display cabinet pp. 24-25
+ 2 strips 45 in x 1½ in

Robot's hand
pp. 18-19

Maze pp. 10-11

Maze pp. 10-11

Robot's radar
pp. 18-19
cut 2

Perfume display cabinet pp. 24-25
+ 2 strips 45 in x 1½ in

Photography by Sylvie Vernichon

© of the american edition:
Editions Fleurus, Paris, 1997
ISBN: 0-7651-9102-4

© Editions Fleurus, Paris, 1996 for the original edition
Title of the french edition:
Kit Mercredi des Petits, Tout en carton ondulé
English translation by Translate-A-Book, a division of
Transedition Limited, Oxford, England.
Printed in France
Distributor in the USA: SMITHMARK Publishers Inc.
115 west 18th street, New York, NY 10011.
Distributor in Canada: Prologue Inc.
1650 Bd Lionel Bertrand, Boisbriand, Québec J7H4N7.

CREATING WITH
CARDBOARD

Violaine Lamérand

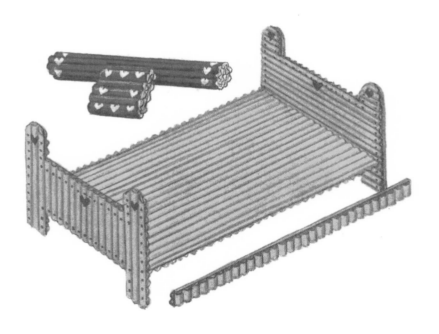

Illustrator: Jean-Pierre Lamérand

FLEURUS

Corrugated cardboard is easy to cut and can be bought by the roll in a huge variety of colors. It comes in several thicknesses, the finest of which is microgrooved corrugated cardboard.

In this book you will also be making models from cardboard boxes and packing cardboard, both of which are made out of double layers of corrugated cardboard. Your models will work best if you carefully follow the direction of the corrugation as shown in the illustrations.

A maze

You will need: lid of a cardboard box • corrugated cardboard •
2 corks • 2 push pins • poster paint • glue • scissors •
2 toothpicks • marbles • a piece of colored paper the same size
as the inside of the box lid • round stickers • templates from the
front of the book

1 Paint the inside of your box lid or cover it with colored paper. Glue a double layer of corrugated cardboard to form a small wall around the edges of the lid.

2 Paint the corks and, when dry, attach them to the outside of the lid at opposite corners (see photograph) using the push pins.

3 Using the templates, cut out two of each of the maze shapes and glue them together. Make sure that the ridges are running in opposite directions on the largest two shapes.

4 Cut out four arrows and glue them together to make two. Slide a toothpick in the middle of each arrow and place them at the start and finish. Write numbers on stickers and use these as scoring areas within the maze.

50

Shadow puppet theater

You will need: a large cardboard carton • red corrugated cardboard • gold paint • sheet of tracing paper (20 in x 24 in) • scissors • **Puppets:** strong black paper • wooden skewers • thread • transparent tape • flashlight or desk lamp

1 **Ask an adult** to cut out a large window from the base of the carton. Cover all the outside of the box with red corrugated cardboard.

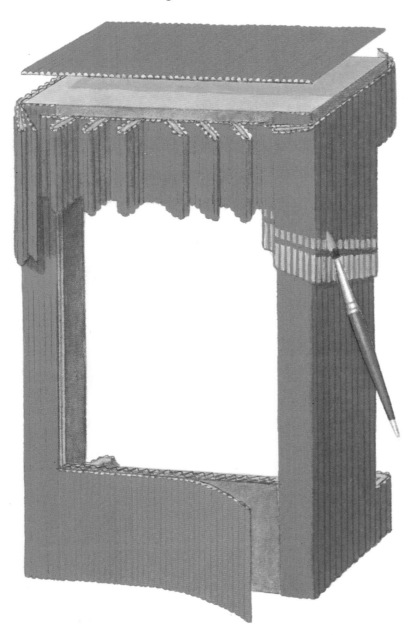

2 Cut another long piece of cardboard to make the curtain at the top of the theater. Shape it as shown in the pictures and fold pleats along the front and sides. Paint a gold fringe along the bottom edge.

3 Cut the tracing paper to fit the window and glue it to the inside of the box. Reinforce this with more strips of corrugated cardboard, stuck around the edge of the window. This can then be used for holding stationary puppets and background objects. Cut out puppet shapes and stick a wooden skewer to the back of each. Shine a light from behind the theater to make the shadows.

Puppets

You will need: corrugated cardboard • glue • feathers • beads • pieces of foam • stapler • paper fastener • templates from the front of the book

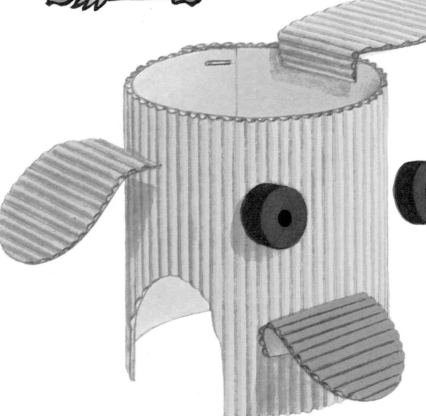

2 To make the dog's muzzle, roll up a strip of cardboard and push out the middle as shown above. Glue inside and add a bead to make the nose.

1 Make a tube of corrugated cardboard and staple it together. Cut a semi-circle out of each side for your thumb and little finger. These scraps can be used to make ears.

Props

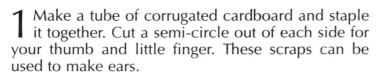

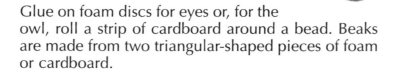

Glue on foam discs for eyes or, for the owl, roll a strip of cardboard around a bead. Beaks are made from two triangular-shaped pieces of foam or cardboard.

Glue a cardboard ring to the props to make them easy to hold. The cat's whiskers can be made by putting together three strips of cardboard with a paper fastener.

A temple timetable

You will need: a rectangular piece of cardboard measuring 16 in x 24 in • white corrugated cardboard • glue • blue paper • ruler • felt-tip pens

1 Cut out a house shape from the cardboard and cover the roof with corrugated cardboard. Draw in the days and times of your timetable on the piece of blue paper, then stick it under the roof area (pediment).

2 Make rolls of corrugated cardboard to fit around the triangle of the pediment, and glue and staple them in place. The ends of the two top rolls should be cut diagonally to fit neatly. Decorate the pediment with some coiled shapes.

capital

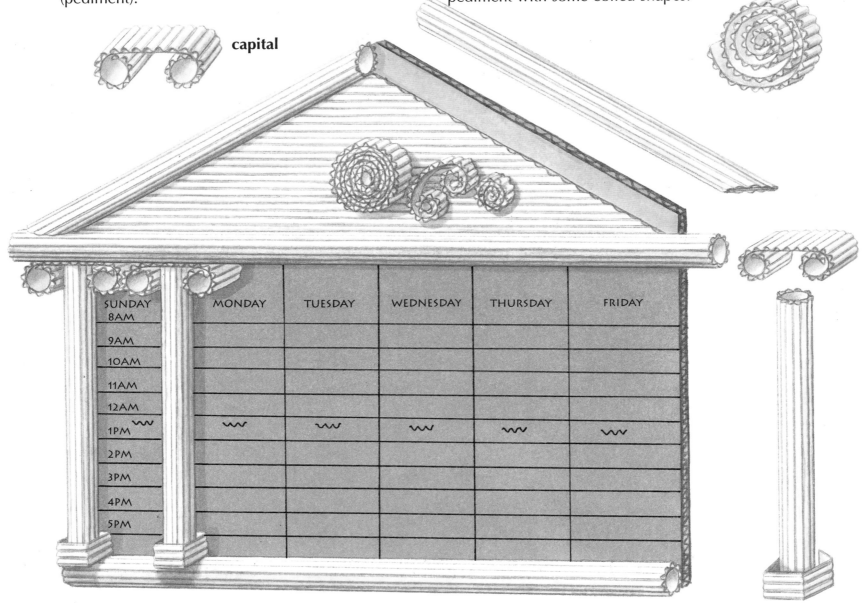

	SUNDAY 8AM	MONDAY	TUESDAY	WEDNESDAY	THURSDAY	FRIDAY
9AM						
10AM						
11AM						
12AM						
1PM						
2PM						
3PM						
4PM						
5PM						

3 Glue a roll of cardboard at the foot of the temple, then measure the distance between the roof and the base. Make seven columns of rolled up cardboard slightly shorter than this distance and stick them at equal intervals on the timetable.

4 Roll up little strips of corrugated cardboard to make capitals and glue one to the top of each column. Glue another strip around the foot of each column. Now your timetable is ready to use – or you could give it as a present to a friend.

Robot night light

You will need: corrugated cardboard in three different colors • glue • cylindrical lampshade frame • 25 paper fasteners • 1 nail • black felt-tip pen • templates from the front of the book

1 Roll a piece of corrugated cardboard around the lampshade frame. Pull it tight and close the tube with paper fasteners. Use a nail to help you make the holes.

2 Cut two strips of cardboard that are larger than the diameter of your cylinder, cross one over the other at the top (see picture) and attach them with paper fasteners. Cut a cardboard circle and place it in the center of the bands. Using the template, cut out two radar shapes and glue them together.

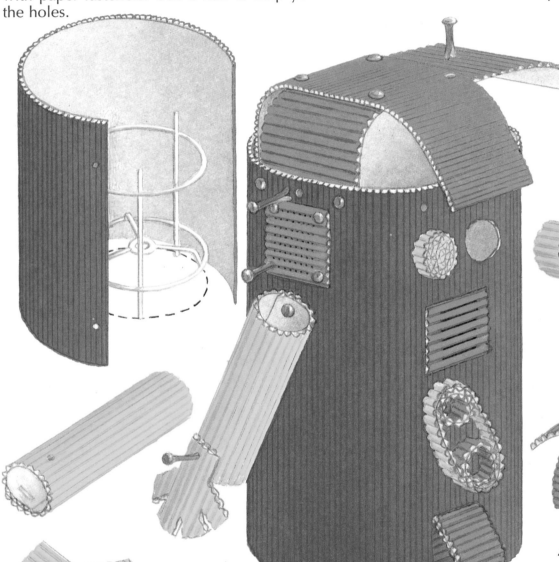

3 Make the arms from two rolls of corrugated cardboard and attach them to the body with paper fasteners. Using the template, cut out two hands and attach them to the end of each arm.

4 Cut holes for the eyes. Roll up two thin strips of corrugated cardboard and place one in each of the eyeholes. Glue a strip of cardboard at the foot of the robot, attaching it front and back to look like a wheel. Make some decorative cogs and grills to stick to the robot and pierce some ventilation holes in the sides. **Ask an adult** to place a lamp inside your robot. The bulb should be no stronger than 25 watts.

Dollhouse living room

You will need: corrugated cardboard • scissors • glue • ruler •
Armchair: 1 strip 24 in x 3 in (back and sides) • 2 strips 4 in x
2 in (armrests) • 4 strips ½ in x 4 in (feet)

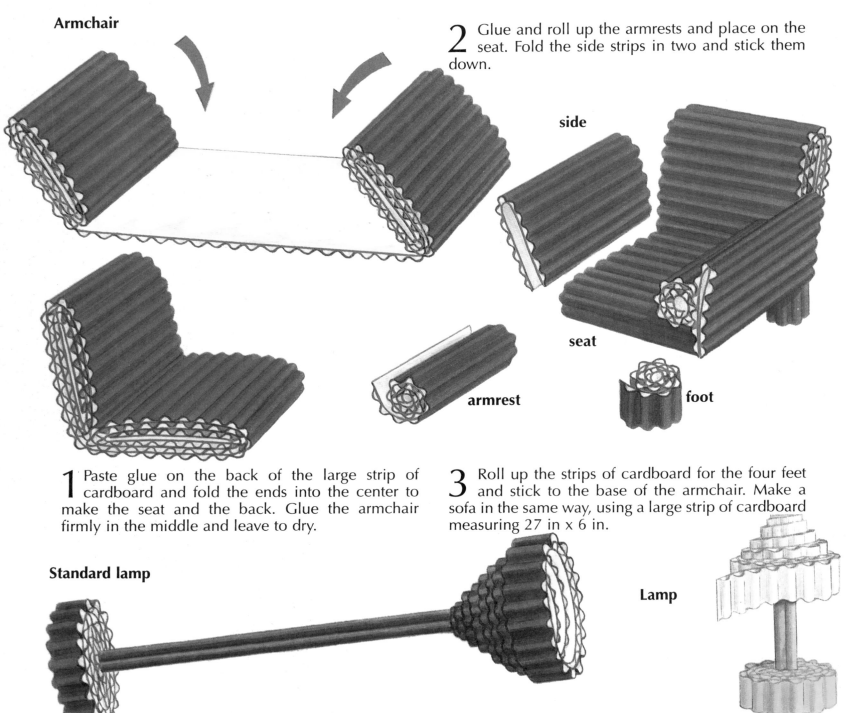

Armchair

2 Glue and roll up the armrests and place on the seat. Fold the side strips in two and stick them down.

side

seat

armrest

foot

1 Paste glue on the back of the large strip of cardboard and fold the ends into the center to make the seat and the back. Glue the armchair firmly in the middle and leave to dry.

3 Roll up the strips of cardboard for the four feet and stick to the base of the armchair. Make a sofa in the same way, using a large strip of cardboard measuring 27 in x 6 in.

Standard lamp

Lamp

Paste glue on the back of two long, narrow strips and roll them around either end of a rod made from corrugated cardboard. Make the lampshade by pushing out the center of the top strip before the glue dries.

Dollhouse bedroom

You will need: corrugated cardboard • red poster paint • 2 paper fasteners • scissors • glue • templates from the back of the book

Wardrobe

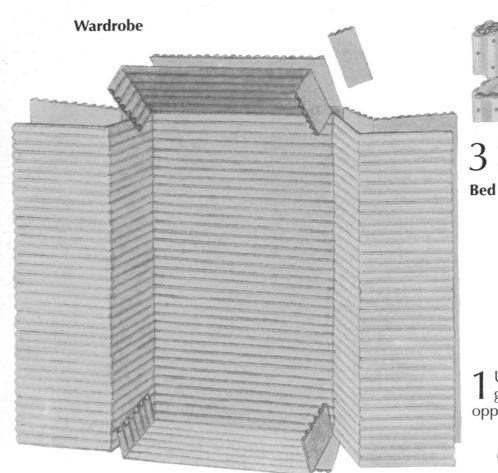

3 Glue down the top of the wardrobe. Make some shelves and slide them between the ridges.

Bed

1 Using the template, cut out two headboards and glue them together making sure the ridges run in opposite directions. Do the same for the foot of the bed.

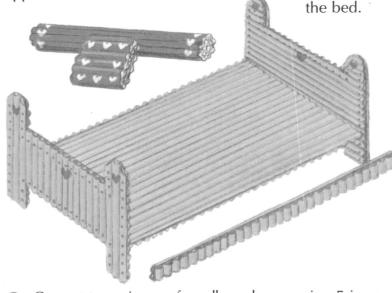

1 Using the template, cut out two wardrobe shapes and glue them together making sure the ridges run at right angles to each other. Remove the small flaps from the cardboard with the vertical ridges (as shown above). Fold along the dotted line and glue the flaps to the inside.

2 Cut out two hearts and attach to the wardrobe doors with paper fasteners. Place a thin strip of cardboard behind one heart to make a bolt.

2 Cut out two pieces of cardboard measuring 5 in x 8 in and glue them in the same way to form the mattress. Fit the mattress between the headboard and foot. Glue a strip of corrugated cardboard along each side of the bed.

Display cabinet

You will need: a sheet of corrugated packing cardboard • colored paper for the base • colored corrugated cardboard • glue • 2 adhesive strips • string • pins • scissors • templates from the front and back of the book

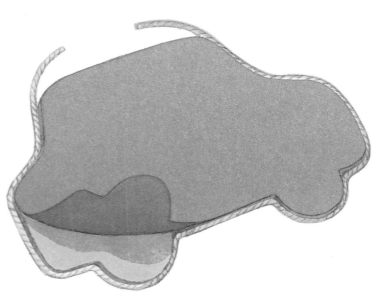

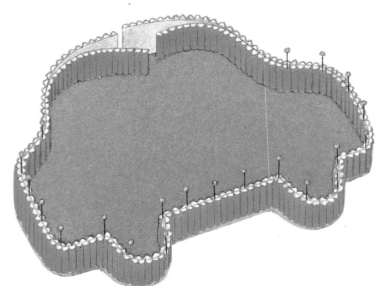

1 Choose your template and cut the shape out of corrugated packing cardboard. Cover it with colored paper and measure the circumference with a piece of string.

2 Use the string to cut two strips of cardboard with a width of 1½ in. Stick these back to back, leaving an overlap of ¾ in, with the ridges running the same way on both sides. Glue this around the base, securing with pins until it dries.

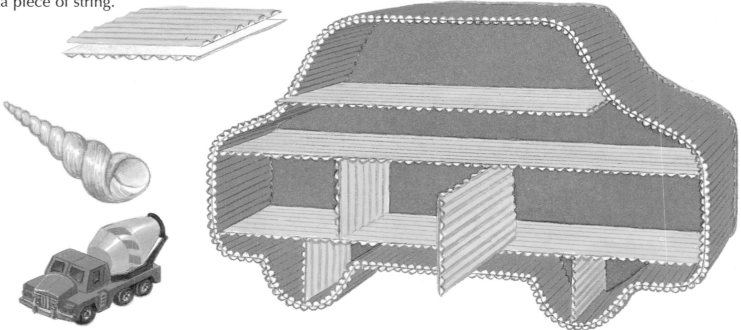

3 Now make some partitions. Cut two pieces of cardboard for each partition, gluing them back to back with the ridges running in opposite directions to make the cardboard stiffer. Cut each partition to the right length and slide into place along the ridges. Attach two adhesive strips to the back of the cabinet. You could secure your display objects inside with a reusable adhesive.

A desk caddy

You will need: a small cardboard box • corrugated cardboard in various colors • 2 large empty matchboxes • 4 in of cord • glue • scissors • ruler

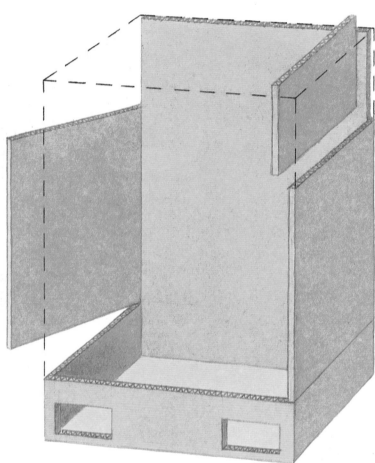

1 **Ask an adult** to cut up a small box as shown above, including the holes in the front where you will slide in the matchboxes as drawers.

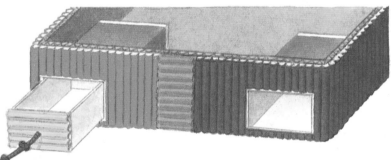

2 Glue the outer bottom of each matchbox to the base of the box. Thread each drawer with a piece of cord, knot and slide into position. Then cover all sides of the box with corrugated cardboard (see large photograph).

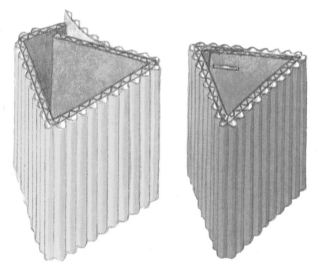

3 Using scraps cut from the cardboard box, make triangular-shaped pencil containers, as shown above, and stick these to the base of the desk caddy.

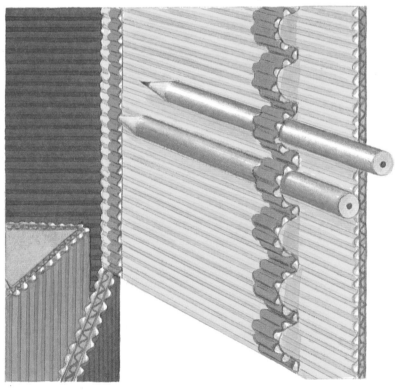

4 Cut two long thin strips of corrugated cardboard to make the pencil holder and glue to the front flap. Make little arches in the outer strip for the pencils, as shown above.

A merry-go-round

You will need: corrugated cardboard • sheet of cardboard • round cardboard cheese box • 2 wooden skewers • air-drying modeling clay • paperclip • half a toilet roll tube • thread • scissors • glue • templates from the back of the book.

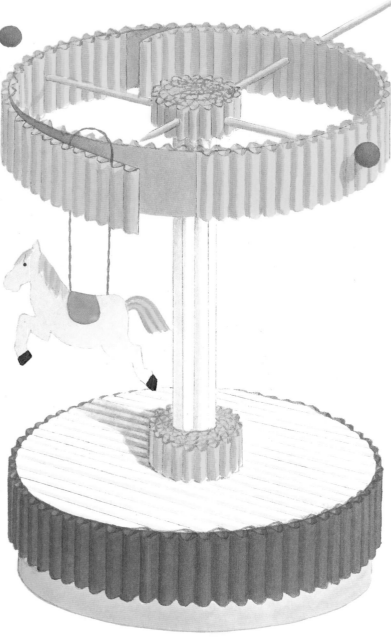

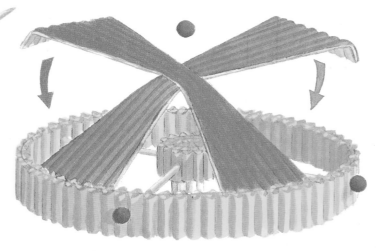

2 Break off the ends of the skewers and fix with modeling clay. Using the template, cut two roof pieces and staple to the circle.

3 Fill the toilet roll tube with corrugated cardboard and cover the outside. Unbend the paperclip as shown and put a piece of modeling clay on one end to make the crank. Push the hooked end into the filled tube.

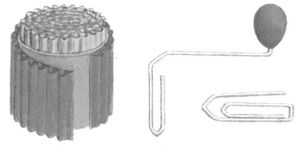

1 Cover the cheesebox lid. Make a central pole 7 in high from rolled-up card, then roll two more strips (³⁄₄ in x 14 in) around each end of the pole. Push the skewers through the top roll so that they intersect at right angles, as shown. Cut two more strips of card (1¼ in x 20 in) and glue back to back. Attach this in a circle around the skewers.

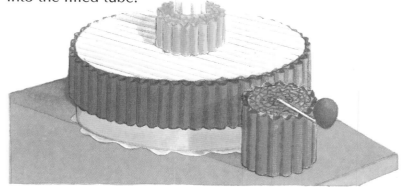

4 Put the lid on the cheesebox and glue the bottom. Place the crank next to this so it can act as a cog wheel. Cut out and hang four horses.